Into the Beautiful

Journeys

Poetry by Montana Artists

S. E. Thomas, M.A., Editor

**Into the Beautiful
Journeys**
Poetry by Montana Artists
Volume IV

S. E. Thomas, M.A., Editor

Published by The Dramatic Pen Press, L.L.C.

Lolo, Montana

Cover Image Taken by S. E. Thomas
at Two Medicine Lake
Glacier National Park

A great many thanks to the hardworking

English and literature teachers across our beautiful state.

May your legacy of beauty continue to flourish

long after we are gone.

Table of Contents

Our Winners

Adult Poetry Contest Winners

First Place

Life's Journey

Many curves and switchbacks,
Long and boring straightaways,
Random construction slow downs
And bumps ahead –
Days that are sunny and clear,
Nights where lightning reveals the storm,
Evenings when the visor shades
My eyes from the sun –
Long, slow mountain climbs,
Windy routes 'long streams and rivers,
Countless scenes and ways
All taking me
Homeward
To that safe, quiet rest.

Al Leland

About the Author

Allen E. Leland was born in Waukegan, IL, to parents who were both teachers. Leland, having taught in Montana 30 plus years, is currently at Lustre Christian High School. He enjoys camping, hunting, and fishing. He also loves spending time with family, especially his wife Connie and son Tom.

Second Place

Answers

I had not considered it before,

about birds on a wire.

One departs, another arrives,

others shift positions.

Each striving to maintain stability.

Like birds on a wire,

we too struggle to remain upright during the

transitions of life.

The answer may not be in the flight,

but in the holding on tight.

Augusta Nichols

About the Author

The author was raised on a small ranch in Montana. She is a wife, mother, grandmother, and great-grandmother. She is the past Vice-President of the Lewistown Arts & Entertainment District and is a member of the Lewistown Writers' Group. Her first book, *My Garden*, was featured in 'State of the Arts,' the Montana Arts Council's quarterly publication.

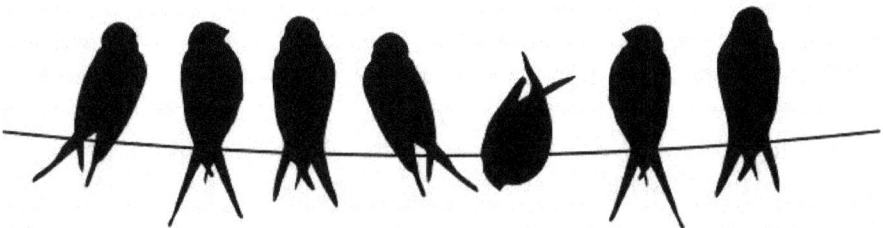

Third Place

a country road

it's a gravel road
and the gravel is at once taunting and yet forgiving
giving the tires a little cushion and yet tearing them away
holding them loosely, letting them ride the turns
and dance along with the motor as it rises and falls
and yet, the road is always ready to let go
it won't let the car dance alone, they must be together

it's a river road
and it flows beneath you
and it wants you to ride the waves, not to conquer them
it takes you up and sends your headlights into the night sky
and drops out from under you
waiting to see if you've let your mind get too far away
but it's ready to catch you if you're ready to land –
or catch you off guard if you lose the rhythm

it's a country road
it's a way home
and it loves to dance.

Geoff Smith

About the Author

Geoff Smith grew up travelling Montana's highways and backroads. Between family trips as a child and his own driving for work and pleasure, he has been in every county of Montana, and personally driven through all but one. He spends his winters teaching science and part of his summers with tour groups in and around Yellowstone Park and southwest Montana. The shortest distance between two points may be a straight line, but the most interesting trip between two places in Montana is an untraveled route, and Geoff seldom passes up a chance to take a new road.

Teen Poetry Contest Winner

First Place

The Flight, The Flightless

Birds,
upon birds,
upon birds.
As they line the seashore,
as they circle their prey like a noose,
and dive down like light into deep water,
and settle on tree branches like the moon resting between rolling hills.
And they are a breath caught by the wind,
and they are a crescendo of flapping wings
when the bells toll,
and every early morning a harmony is born.

It's like this when you wake up in the dark,
or hear your name called in the distance but there is nobody around.
An echo,
a memory you never thought of before,
but it's the one you wake up to.

And in dim sunlight you drink your tea,
and watch the birds fall and be caught again,
and they warble and peck
at the pain you tried to forget.

Claire Parsons

About the Author

Claire Parsons is a junior in high school with a passion. An avid backpacker and reader, she lives happily in Missoula, Montana.

Second Place

Obsession

I didn't understand why I began,
my obsession to write, to let it out.
Expressing each feeling I held inside,
Turning such simple words into stories...
Stories that wouldn't be complete without you.
Writing should be full of life, energized.
But no, those happy feelings didn't drive me.
The way you told me no, that it wasn't me,
But that it was you and selfish desire...
The way you broke my heart put me in gear.
Sadness drove me mad, yet kept me on track.
Confusion rode in the passenger seat,
While my heart sank in the middle of them...
Scared to drive or ride with, indecisive.
Anger rode in back, begging me to join.
My heart keeps turning left, right, even back.
Staring directly into the unknown...
Unsure of what to decide, so I don't.
My heart takes over, controlling those who are unsure:
sadness, confusion, anger.

Aubrey Larson

About the Author

I'm a senior from Shelby High School. I have a passion for writing, and I really enjoy discovering other works of writing that inspire me.

Third Place

Family Pictures

Family pictures cover my walls
Smiling faces look upon a bright future
Mother and Father full of love for one another
Brother and sister content with life
Don't you know those are five years old?
Family pictures lay at my feet
Smiling faces ripped to shreds
Mother and Father torn apart
Brother and sister questioning life
Every picture shows of what was and what could've been
They show what I've lost
And what I'll never get back

Tana Campbell

About the Author

My name is Tana Campbell, I'm 15 and a sophomore at Hellgate High School. In life we experience the good and the bad. I try to convey those experiences in my writing.

Child Poetry Contest Winner

First Place

The Kind Woman In Autumn

Gracefully she removes her fiery cloak
to warm the frozen townsfolk below her,
She contrasts beautifully with the cloudy backdrop
in her well-taken fall pictures,
This kindly woman welcomes her best friends home
with slightly barer arms than when they left,
She is still young, not prepared to carry
energetic children on her back,
But she generously welcomes them
to gather at her feet, despite her weariness,
As the temperature drops and cold winds
wrench the last leaves from her shivering body,
She drops to sleep, yet to awake
with renewed energy next spring.

Emmy Fanguy

About the Author

Emmy (12) is the oldest child in her family. She loves exploring nature and was inspired by the Mission Mountains to write her poem. Emmy was born in Starkville, Mississippi and moved to Missoula, Montana when she was four. Emmy loves reading, writing, and creating art (including Chinese Calligraphy). Emmy has developed a recent love for China, as God has placed on her heart the dream of being a missionary. Emmy has two pets, Sweet Pea (dog) and Samson (guinea pig). Her parents are Joe and Kari, and her siblings are Preston (8) Madelynn (7) Ethan (3) and Lillian (2).

Second Place

The Journey of My Fears

Spinning. Spiders. Sharks.
Dreams that seem too real.
Lost. A labyrinth.
Who's that at my bedroom door?
My imagination.
Carousels. No sleep. Loneliness.
When my dog isn't there when I get home.
Politics. Too much blood. Falling.
Dreams that seem too real.
Dizziness. Thorns. Nausea.
When the world stops spinning.
Somehow I still feel dizzy.

Sydney Yung

About the Author

My name is Sydney Yung, and I am in 6th grade and go to Sussex School. I love theater, animals, art, and of course writing! I have two Bernese Mountain/Golden Retriever mixes named Maggie and Kumma. My worst fear is Spiders. Well, to be fair, I do have Arachnophobia. When I grow up I want to be –no, I will be, an actress.

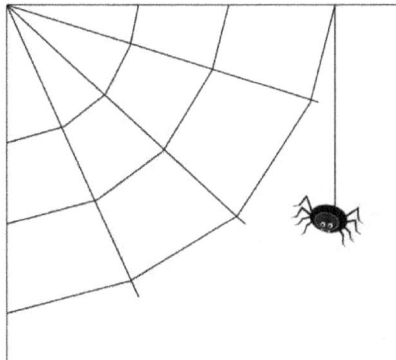

Third Place

Journey to Everest

I wedge my frostbitten body into the crevasse in the Hillary step,
the wind tears at my hands and feet.

As I wedge my hands into the rock and start to climb,
the rock starts to feel like cold iron rubbing on my ice cold palms.

As I heave my body over the top.
I see my partner's cold, blue face lying stiffly in the snow,

the life slowly trickling from his pale blue face.

I notice that I am on the tallest mountain in the world
without a living soul in sight.

Elliot Laroche

About the Author

My name is Elliott Laroche. I like to ski, play hockey, and write about climbing. I am 12 and attend Sussex School.

Poems by Adults

The Other Side

the other side of the river
appears far away
beyond reach
I long to be there by the water's edge
near the stark trees
looking back at me
I would brave the icy waters
for my desire is all consuming
to not be here
but to be there
in the clearing by the woods
freedom from my very being
at the water's edge
looking back at me

James Van Ness
Honorable Mention

About the Author

Retired corporate gypsy – BSChE University of North Dakota, MBA University of Connecticut – Montana State University student mentor, poet, hiker, skier, and a lover of great independent film.

Never Let You Go

Wind howling outside, tree branch rubbing on the window.
Scared little girl, hides her head under her pillow.
Daddy peeks on in, says,
"Honey do you hear the wind, blowing through the willows?"
And Daddy holds her tight, says "everything will be alright,"
squeezes her and doesn't want to let go "as you're growing up in life,
everything will be alright, but now is not the time for me to let you go."
Horn honking outside, school bus coming for her first day.
Wrapped around daddy's legs, she don't want to go away.
But daddy says "it's time, everything will be just fine,
you're looking for your big day."
But Daddy holds her tight, says "everything will be alright,"
squeezes her and doesn't want to let go "as you're growing up in life,
everything will be alright, there will come a time for me to let you go."
Pretty white dress, coming down the aisle, with tears in his eyes,
Daddy smiles,
And Daddy holds her tight, says "everything will be alright,"
squeezes her and doesn't want to let go "as you're growing up in life,
everything will be alright, but now is time for me to let you go,
But in my heart, I will never, ever, let you go."

William K. Porta

About the Author

Bill Porta is an avid writer, Father, business owner, and real estate instructor. He teaches Sunday School, Children's Church, and participates in the Celebrate Recovery program as a teacher and mentor.

Questions

thoughts like waterfalls splash and echo

have you ever seen so many blinding shades of green?

look out of a fifth floor window and see just the tops of trees

if you had one wish what would it be?

i wish i knew how long i had within the numbered days

sometimes i try and talk to god

but i always get stuck on what to say

i doubt a god could answer my queries anyway

questions refract trapped in a brain like honeycomb.

Dusty Keim

About the Author

Third year student at the University of Montana studying English Literature and Creative Writing.

Northern Alberta

Northern Alberta
I stand here under the moon howling
like a wolf for its mate
yet the forest is quiet
and does not return my ache
I am numb at minus 37 Centigrade
tears frozen silent against my face
aurora borealis dances across the sky
as the frigid night air clings to everything
seventeen hours of darkness
does nothing to warm the soul

James Van Ness

About the Author

Retired corporate gypsy – BSChE University of North Dakota, MBA University of Connecticut – Montana State University student mentor, poet, hiker, skier and a lover of great independent film.

Rose Blood

Through the powdery forest I follow your little bunny tracks.
Under tree limbs hanging broken and rotting.
Over mounds of fallen boughs,
where your little bunny tracks end
in a pool of bright red bunny blood.
Seeping red into white, pink, coral, rose, shards of fur,
traces of bone.
I see how you must have stopped paralyzed with fear
nose twitching the air, fur blending,
waiting for the death that had found you.
You won't be multiplying this spring.
You are the coyote's breath now, the earth's soil.
You are buried in the wild.
Your graveyard runs free.

Rebecca Bain Patchell

About the Author

I have lived in Whitefish in the same house for about 22 years. Sometimes loving it here and sometimes not, especially in those long, torpedo gray winters. Now I am just here writing when I must and enjoying the end and beginning of each new season.

Highway 200 Blues

Just resting on the shoulders of the highway of my youth;
my trav'ling companion when we were both young;
and dreaming of the mornings when I'd always find some truth
while running away from or into the sun.

The traffic on the highway all too often moves too fast
for people who seldom have somewhere to go.
A ride I might be sharing may just carry me on past
a friend I remember; a place that I know.

The music of the highway is still ringing in my ears;
the sounds of the land or a voice from inside.
It's still the same old songs that we have sung for years and years
- but music is always along for the ride.

Sometimes I'm on the highway and I'm only there to roam
with no destination, the road is a friend.
The highway of my youth is where I'll always feel at home
while travelling toward but not reaching the end.

Geoff Smith

About the Author

Geoff Smith grew up travelling Montana's highways and backroads. Between family trips as a child and his own driving for work and pleasure, he has been in every county of Montana, and personally driven through all but one. He spends his winters teaching science and part of his summers with tour groups in and around Yellowstone Park and southwest Montana. The shortest distance between two points may be a straight line, but the most interesting trip between two places in Montana is an untraveled route, and Geoff seldom passes up a chance to take a new road.

Hannah's Perfect Resting Place

Lovely blessing of light from above

Faithfully living for Jesus

shining bright with God's love

A believer in hope and full of merciful grace

rewarded as He promises

in heaven's perfect resting place

Diane Johnson Cottrell

About the Author

Diane Johnson Cottrell resides in the Bitterroot Valley Montana with her husband Alton, and their Golden Red Retriever, Samuel James. Diane is "re-learning" to live and breathe since the death of her 23 year old daughter and best friend Hannah in an auto accident. She is doing so by writing and journaling thoughts, dreams and memories. This poem is inscribed on the back of Hannah's memorial bench that Diane placed at the Victor Montana Cemetery for those visiting there who need a quiet place to contemplate the journey of their loved one(s).

Happy Valley

Seven hundred fifty-eight miles
To the place where I left you behind;
O'er the green rolling hills,
Through the blackberry briars.
Fifteen years since I drove out of town.
You're still in that same valley now;
That same quiet place,
That same piece of ground.
Twelve hours ten minutes away;
I'd drive out, but what's left to say?
Goodbye is long gone,
And nothing has changed.
A thousand times over it hurts,
But I guess that's just how the world works.
Didn't want to leave you
But, daddy, you left me first.
I still miss you, for what it's worth,
But you left me first.

Katie Powner

About the Author

Katie Powner lives in Manhattan, Montana with her husband, three kids, one cat, and eight chickens. She hopes to one day also have a mini-pig and dress it up in funny, little sweaters.

The Mystery of Time

The seed of time is flawless as it falls to the earth.
Amidst the apple blossoms,
the humming of bees flying from tree to tree.
Let it be Adam said to Eve, you're the apple of my eye.
The coal pressed diamonds are the keys to young girls' hearts,
as he bleeds and pleads on bended knee, why me?
The bread of life, etched in stone, dust to dust, ashes to ashes,
I'll have a slice of life.
Whose to pay the price?
Water mixed with wine,
the well spring of time pressed from grapes.
Fermenting of yeast and grapes create a heavenly feast.
Eat of my flesh, drink of my blood."
Through the hour glass of time sifted by sand,
I'll give you my hand to pass safely through this land.

Jennifer Nicole Uncles

About the Author

My name is Jennifer Nicole Uncles. I was born and raised in Montana. My hobbies are fishing, baking, and cooking. I also enjoy spoiling my nieces and nephews. I have a sense of humor and witty personality, and I love to joke and make others laugh.

Many paths, One road

Sometimes a climb, others a coast.

Sometimes we cry, others we boast.

The path is well planned.

Guided by the masters hand.

This road we follow is a challenge for me.

Trust is the road to where I must be.

Jim Uncles

About the Author

My name is Jim Uncles. I am a native Montanan, born in Butte, Montana. I was raised in Helena, Montana. I am the fourth of seven siblings. I have been married about 38 years, with two sons and a daughter.

So Much More

I lost my right arm today.

A violent severing of my soul.

The wound piercing through my heart.

I am exposed, stripped of my very being.

I often took you for granted,

hardly noticing your presence.

I find myself looking at the

place you once occupied.

I am stunned to find you gone.

I am afraid to do what we once did together.

The pain of loss intense.

How will I survive without you.

Today I lost my right arm.

Today I lost my wife.

Augusta Nichols

About the Author

The author was raised on a small ranch in Montana. She is a wife, mother, grandmother, and great-grandmother. She is the past Vice-President of the Lewistown Arts & Entertainment District and is a member of the Lewistown Writers' Group. Her first book, *My Garden*, was featured in 'State of the Arts,' the Montana Arts Council's quarterly publication.

Poems by Teens

Locked in a Glass Case

I have a life of drowning,
A life of pressure.
No one can see past the frowning,
But yet I sit on top of a dresser.

Locked in a glass case,
Not yet shattered but also not whole.
Sometimes I can see a familiar face,
They tap the glass hard enough to takes its toll,

I used to have another friend locked away with me,
Drowning, they didn't mind being here locked up
Until he went belly up.

They scooped him up with a swish
Never to been seen again,
They didn't seem to care,
But then again we are just fish.

Ashlie Potter
Honorable Mention

About the Author

Hi, my name is Ashlie. I am 16 and I enjoy writing. I'm actually going to study to become a writer.

Run Away

Far away from home, my life miles away
New start, new family
Fake smile, happy friends
Dark nights, drunken rage
Neighbors turn a blind eye from the cries
Run away from the rage, only to have a heart pull you back
Fake smile, happy friends
Dark nights, drunken rage
911 what's your emergency?
New life packed up, new family gone
Fake smile, everything's fine
Back home, new school
Outcast, dark nights
Sad eyes, happy smile
Tear stains, bruised wrists
You ok?
Breakdown, new truths
Broken heart resurfaced and buried again
Fake smile, happy friends
Is everything ok now?

Tana Campbell
Honorable Mention

About the Author

My name is Tana Campbell. I'm 15 and a sophomore at Hellgate High School. In life we experience the good and the bad. I try to convey those experiences in my writing.

A Journey Home

I am just a girl
who is not accepted
Fake smiles help me get through the day
To try and ignore the thought of me being unkept
I am afraid to be myself
Afraid of being destroyed
My friends want me to open up
The thought of that makes me paranoid
I need to be brave
I need to be strong
I will not let them define me
I have to prove these people wrong
I am just a girl
On a journey home
To find my place in this world
Even if it requires me to be alone

Faith Amber Stenger

About the Author

My name is Faith, I am sixteen years old, and I am from Shelby, Montana. I enjoy writing, reading, and music. In my free time you can either find me in a silent place writing a new story, poem. song or reading novels.

Rewind

Why did I say the word love
Why did you walk away
Closing the door
Leaving me on the floor, alone
Why did I say the word love
Rewind the clock
Back to the moments before
Before I was alone
Before you closed the door
Before you walked away
Before I said the word love
Back to a simpler love
Rewind the clock
Take me back is all I ask
Why did I say the word love
I want to take it back
I can't deny the feeling, but I can take the words back
I can wait
Rewind the clock
Take me back, is all I ask

Tana Campbell

About the Author

My name is Tana Campbell. I'm 15 and a sophomore at Hellgate High School. In life we experience the good and the bad. I try to convey those experiences in my writing.

Rough Waters

Life ain't always easy, But those perfect lives seem cheesy.
Those Hollywood actors are fake - they pretend for their own sake.
And life ain't always fair,
But those people who don't make mistakes, they don't care -
About people, about things, they just take what life brings.
But to survive in this world, you have to feel.
Because that passion - it's real.
You need emotions, so live in the moment.
You're not a wanna be - you're what you want to be.
And sure, you're gonna have those ups and downs.
Those tear soaked frowns.
But you're also gonna have the smiles,
and the love and the laughter.
Because after, only after the storm there is a rainbow.
It's like navigating through rough waters on the open sea.
And people may call you crazy for choosing your own journey,
But hey, life ain't always easy.

Sarah A. Caffrey

About the Author

I'm 14 years old, I'm from Shelby, Montana, and I found my love of poetry in my 8th grade English class when my teacher, Mr. Hill. He made me write my first poem ever and encouraged me to keep writing.

The Journey of Odysseus

His journey took him far and near
Over a big expanse of blue
He sailed nights and days, days and nights
Hoping to one day return
For ten years, he fought, and ten years he sailed
Hoping to find the right trail
Along the way, if he had known,
He would've sailed faster.
For men had taken his house for their own
And had taken over his pasture
He wouldn't have dallied with beauties and flowers
Nor blinded men who displeased him
Instead he would've sailed for hours
To give his wife her freedom
But now he's home
With his people
Leading a life of great
Never again will he leave his house
Or ever pass the gate

Marie Sainsbury

About the Author

My name is Marie Sainsbury. I am 14 years old, live in Missoula, Montana, and love to write. I decided to enter a poem as part of an English assignment, and because it looked like fun. My favorite past times are running with friends, biking, going to school, and reading.

"Fly Maria Fly"

I grasped her mane tightly.

And closed my eyes.

For she was old.

And was

About to die.

I hopped on her back.

She began to fly.

To heaven we were headed. I started to cry.

The horse slowed down. I was still crying.

She started galloping.

We were not flying. I woke up in shock.

It was just a dream. I looked at the clock.

But I just couldn't believe. I woke up in shock.

It was just a dream. I glanced at the clock.

Then I was crying.

The journey we took that night was one I won't forget.

Rylan Ruth Signalness

About the Author

When my first horse passed away, I couldn't stop thinking about her. Even though this was horrible for me, this poem helped me move on and keep riding the race of life.

Summiting Snowyside Pass

Good news,
its lunchtime
and we've reached
the top of the mountain.

Good news,
all the whitebark pine trees
are alive up here,
and the longer you live
the more likely you'll live longer.

Good news.
The newspaper doesn't come
to our house anymore,
we read it online.
We've been running out of rubber bands.

I can see ranges of batholithic rock,
moraines, and tiny tired hikers
making their way across these great divides.

Good news, sit down,
its lunchtime.

Claire Parsons

About the Author

Claire Parsons is a junior in high school with a passion. An avid backpacker and reader, she lives happily in Missoula, Montana.

Life

Life is a road that we all have to travel,
For some the road's long,
For others, quite short.
In this road there are many bends,
And none know when it will end,

Yet through it all we know,

For some the day's hard and cold,
For some the day's warm and gold.
For some troubles are many,
For others, troubles are few.

Yet through it all we know,

Somewhere someone's living,
Somewhere someone's dying.
Somewhere someone's laughing,
Somewhere someone's crying.

Yet through it all we know, Hard as it may be,

At the end of this road that we see,
There's a beautiful place for you and for me,
A place where our sorrows will become none,
A place where eternally we'll live with the One.

Sarah Rye

About the Author

Since Sarah was a young child, she has aspired to become a writer. Her gift with words became evident as she competed in and won the Treasure State Spelling Bee in 2016. Sarah is well traveled, having visited over half the states in America. With her family, she moved to Montana three years ago and quickly came to love living in an area where she can both go for a quiet woodland hike out her back door any day of the year and drop in on friends in town at a moment's notice.

Poems by Children

The Journey

Cold
Little Steps
Inch by inch
Marvelous
Big mountain
I am falling
Never doing this again
Gigantic challenge

Tooting (scared farting)
Help me, Mom
Every time I fall I get back up

Momma bear,
Oh my gosh, I am scared
Up and up,
Never doing this again
Take me home
Always falling down this mountain
I am terrified
Not my fault I can't climb

Braelynn Mangold, Age 10
Honorable Mention

About the Author

Hello, my name is Braelynn. I am in fifth grade. I am ten years old. I am from Superior, but I was born in Missoula. I love horses. I wrote my poem because I like to be funny. I also like bears. I want to thank you for taking the time to read my poem. I can't wait for you to read it!

The Journey of Hunting Rights

She hits the ground.
Blood splatters.
Her eyes go wide, petrified.
She paws the earth struggling to get up.
Her back goes numb.
She lays there still.
Do you like hunting?
I don't.
Bullets.
Blood.
Taking innocent lives.
Think how you would feel if animals went around with guns
and shot us off one by one
until there's nothing left but dust and bones.
But we shoot them on a daily basis, and it's no big deal.
Why do we think we are better?
Better than them.
Why?
Why?

Ella Simon, Age 11
Honorable Mention

About the Author

Hi! My name is Ella. I go to Sussex School in Missoula and I am 11. I LOVE Animals!!!!! I horseback ride, act, do art, play soccer, dance, write, and I love music! I have two dogs, (that I love to train!), a sister, and a Mom and Dad.

Nature

Trees growing high, growing high.
Birds chirping loud for all to hear,
Flying south for winter.
Coming back in summer, seeing wildlife all the time.
Coyotes' singing let you know summer is coming,
Bears growling to let everyone know
that they want the fresh
huckleberries of this year.
Gigantic fish jumping the waterfalls,
Golden eagles grabbing them up to eat them alive.
What a wonderful sight!

Wally Crosby
Honorable Mention

About the Author

My name is Wally Crosby. I'm in the 5th grade, and I'm 11 and 8 months old. I'm from Missoula, MT. I'm an amazing artist, and I like graffiti.

Changes

I run and run but I can't escape it.

I want it to change, but it will not make the deal.

It finds me every time no matter where I go.

I guess I need to deal with who I am and not try to run away.

Changes are journeys for you and I.

Joseph M. Wood, Age 10
Honorable Mention

About the Author

My name is Joseph. I was born in Waxahutchee, Texas and moved to Superior, Montana. I am in 5th grade. My favorite subject is math. I hope my poems get in the book so the other kids and adults can read them. Thank you.

Montana, Sweet Home and Mirthful Journey

Montana, Sweet Home Rivers
ever abundant where bison roam.
Our beautiful Montana, a place we call our home.
Plains of beauty, mountains of grace.
Shining eyes of a joyful face.
Oh love and protect these treasures,
whilst we journey here and there.
Many shall come back to the place of our own.
Mirthful Journey Starting on the journey ahead,
prepared in heart and mind.
Wherever the path may go ahead, though twists and wind.
I start ahead with joyful mirth,
while the sun sings songs upon the earth.
Veil of mist on the earth unwordly, yet true.
Dawn disappears to azure blue.
Myths and legends of bison,
and rivers ever abundant flowing.
Where horses gallop and people go a-rowing.
MONTANA! The place of love.

Jenna Survoy, Age 11
Honorable Mention

About the Author

I'm Jenna Survoy, I live here in Montana. Even though I'm only eleven, I enjoy writing. I'm inspired by our beautiful mountains; I only need to look outside for words. This is my first poetry contest! I live with my two brothers and my mom and dad. I have a typewriter that I write poems and stories on.

Memories

The crunching of leaves under my feet in the fall,
Reminds me of when I was small.
The crunching sound is like the tune to a song;
The peaceful sound of memories.
Reminds me of ocean waves
Lapping at the shore;
Returning evermore.
It is so awesome to hear,
Let's do it again next year.

By Timothy Norling
Honorable Mention

About the Author

I am a fifth grader who enjoys target shooting, archery, building models, bowling, golfing, basketball, hunting, writing, laughing, and my family. I have written and illustrated two books titled: "Don't Let the Peacock Cook Dinner" and "Don't Let the Peacock Drive a Car." The books help kids see it is okay to ask for help.

Journey of a Boy's Racing Heart

From the bag that it is kept, I take it out.
It's cold for it's been waiting to fly for a long time.
As I take it outside it gets colder.
When I reach the twenty yard mark,
it's time to knock it so it can fly.
Then swiftly I pull back. I aim. I let it fly.
The next time it moves, it's late at night.
We move into hunting camp.
It sits a few more hours and then it's time.
I pull it out.
We go miles together, and when the times comes, it will fly again.
But for now there's more hiking to be done. Up the hill we go.
By the time we hit the top, it's been awhile.
Luckily the elk are still bugling.
As if it was seconds later, there, 30 yards in front of me,
stood the biggest bull elk I've ever seen.
The journey was beginning, as I took it from my quiver.
I knocked as I drew back.
I stood still and leveled myself.
Then I let the ARROW fly.

John Kelly
Honorable Mention

About the Author

My name is John Kelly I attend Sussex School in Missoula, Montana. I am a football player and love to hunt and fish and be outdoors.

Aging Fears

Cats, Dark, Eyes
movement that you think you see

Time, Space, Death
The hand that grabs your foot

Age, Night, Falling
Last breath

Progress, Failure, Drained
The noise that you never heard

Birth, Job, Health
The loan that you never paid back

Nicholas Braun, Age 11
Honorable Mention

About the Author

My name is Nicholas Braun. I am 11 years old. I go to Sussex school and like playing soccer. I like to ski in the winter. I have a dog named Sonny.

Rock Journey

River rushing fast

Stone tumbles down roaring creek

Journey to the sea

Abigail Wheeler
Honorable Mention

About the Author

Hi, I'm Abigail Violet Wheeler. I'm 10 years old and was born in Willow Creek, California. I currently live in Superior, Montana, go to Superior Elementary, and I am in 5th grade. I love to write, read, and draw. Also, I'm really glad I entered the poem contest!

Journey Through Memories

Memories,
the ones to forget
Buried deep inside
Of everyone
Forgotten and left alone
To be found one day
Or not
Happy, Sad, Normal,
But, Still forgotten
Memories,
The ones to remember
Easy to find
Inside everyone
Loved and hated
To be forgotten one day
Or still remembered
From hatred
To happiness
To embarrassment
But still, remembered.

Eve Omura, Age 11
Honorable Mention

About the Author

My name is Eve. I'm 11 years old. I go to Sussex school, and I love guinea pigs.

Fears Of a 5 Year Old (The Journey Of a Toddler)

The monster under my bed. My parents yelling at me.
The fact that Jessica will be a copycat
and wear the same dress as me to Maizy's party.
The world coming to an end.
Getting abducted by aliens.
My dog dying.
My brother popping my doll's head off like he said he would.
Reading a chapter book.
Having no friends.
Starting first grade.
My parents being mad at me for breaking their lamp (not my fault).
Talking to adults.
Falling off the chairlift while skiing.
The middle of the night. Bad dreams.
My dog turning into a monster and taking over the world.
That all my fears will suddenly come true and the world
will come to an abrupt end in about five minutes
while my parents are yelling at me.
Meanwhile my brother is popping my doll's head off
(and, no, I am not procrastinating.)

Ila Bell

About the Author

My Name is Ila Bell. I live in Missoula, Montana and attend Sussex School. I like theater, film, art, and soccer. I also play two instruments: piano and drums. I love to write stories and especially poems!

Journey into an Alien Ship

I was walking at night.
While I was walking I felt a crisp wind shift.
I started to feel a tingle in my hands so I started to run home.
A bright light hit my face.
I looked up. I was scared. It looked like a spaceship.
A tube came down and sucked me up.
My hair was so frazzled I looked like I was a troll.
It was all white and clean inside the ship.
I looked over and I saw a control area.
I pressed a weird looking button.
I felt the ship start to spin so I pressed it again.
And it stopped.
But I was so dizzy I accidentally pressed another button.
Then the floor disappeared and, as soon as I knew it, I was falling.
I was so lucky. I fell right on my trampoline.
Then I walked out like it was just another day.

Ryan Maeve Howell

About the Author

Hello! My name is Ryan. I am one of 8 sixth grade girls at Sussex school. I love to make funny videos and hang out with my friends! I also love to mountain bike, ski, and do gymnastics!

The Worst Vacation Ever

Ok
Summer break is supposed to be fun.
You are supposed to hang with friends
and go to Hawaii with grandparents or cousins.
Not go to a country club
with only adults.
Everything is off limits to kids.
Of course, my dad thinks
it will be good fun
to go to a country club.
It's a five hour drive.
So my mom
and my dad
plus my six year old sister
my fifteen year old brother
and, of course, me
all get in the car to go.
But the worst is yet to come.
It's on my 12th birthday.

Seth Iudicello, Age 11

About the Author

My name is Seth. I have two siblings and a dog. I play soccer and I ski during the winter. I am 11 years old and I go to Sussex School.

Utah Backpacking Trip

I was ten years old. I went on a journey across a trail in Utah.
A back-packing trip.
I was with my whole family: my mom, sister, and dad.
We had driven to Moab, Utah, and we went to a trailhead
where we started our backpack journey.
It started out like this: We were hiking, hiking, hiking
for what felt like forever.
Dad looked at the map and said,
"one more mile, then we are at camp, sweet camp."
This went on for the next day. I felt hot and sweaty from the heat,
tired and achy from all the miles walked, and hangry from lack of food.
We reached camp, and then I found out we were staying
for two nights not just one. We had one day to rest.
I woke up to a little doe on the tents. We got up and we made breakfast.
My sister helped my mom make coffee,
and I helped my dad make breakfast.
That night I slept good and had more energy for the walk back to the car.
We got back to the car and packed up.
We drove to go meet our grandparents at a campground
and tell them our whole story.

Eliza Quackenbush

About the Author

My name is Eliza Quackenbush, and I go to Sussex school in Missoula, MT. I love to play hockey and ski in the winter and play soccer and horseback ride in the summer.

Journey To Mexico

It started early
A car ride away from home
Lights shone brightly in the distance
And yet I was still nervous for
A fun and exciting journey ahead
There was still little light
As we entered the plane
It was almost relaxing watching the world
Disappear into the distance
Sleep crept away from tired and exhausted body
But After what seemed like forever
The world came back into view
I stumbled off the plane
Steam filled the doorway and humidity swept over me
That one step out of the airport and I could already see
Twisted vines and green leaves
Tweeting birds
But - sadly - It was over
Just as fast as it had begun
The trip - the journey was over …

Eve Omura, Age 11

About the Author

My name is Eve Omura and I'm 11 years old. I go to Sussex School and I love art. I have 3 amazing guinea pigs, Hat Trick Ryan Omura, Hershy Jelly Belly Omura, and Tasmanian Devil Skunk Omura.

Majesty

Craggy peaks,
Crevices, valleys, hidden paths,
Drop of snow,
Behold Him

Emmy Claire Fanguy

About the Author

Emmy (12) is the oldest child in her family. She loves exploring nature and was inspired by the Mission Mountains to write her poem. Emmy was born in Starkville, Mississippi and moved to Missoula, Montana when she was four. Emmy loves reading, writing, and creating art (including Chinese Calligraphy). Emmy has developed a recent love for China, as God has placed on her heart the dream of being a missionary. Emmy has two pets, Sweet Pea (dog) and Samson (guinea pig). Her parents are Joe and Kari, and her siblings are Preston (8) Madelynn (7) Ethan (3) and Lillian (2).

The Pine

The pine does not eat,
but drinks fresh water

Madelynn Fanguy, Age 7

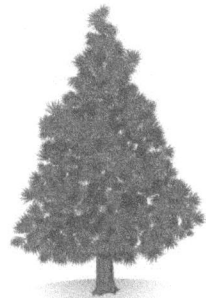

About the Author

Madelynn is 7 years old and loves nature. She is the middle child, with two brothers and two sisters. Madelynn is homeschooled.

The Halloween Ghoul

The ghost is on the run
I bet he is having much fun!
He goes to the forest. He jumps,
Lands on his rump with a big
Thump. He goes home with a huge bump.

Addison Martin, Age 10

About the Author

Hello, my name is Addi. I'm in fifth grade. I'm originally from North Ogden, Utah. I really enjoy holding snakes and my snake. Also, I like reptiles and all animals. I love my farm also.

Life's a Journey

Standing Still, Waiting

Flying, Watching, Sitting

The Life Still Goes On

Finding Its Needs

Heron

Heather Haskins, Age 10

About the Author

Hello, my name is Heather Haskins. I'm in fifth grade and I am the age of ten. I was born in Missoula but live in Torkio and go to school in Superior, MT. I live on a ranch with a bunch of horses, which are my favorite animals. I like writing things and poems are one of my favorite. When I write poems my hands go free and write what they want with some help from my head.

I'm Too Lazy

I'm sitting on the couch, and I'm starting to get hungry,

But the kitchen is SO far away.

But I'm gonna have to get there, so I can stuff my face.

'Cause if I don't, I think I might die.

I finally stand up, but now I have to WALK.

This is gonna be hard. I don't think I'll make it.

I'm almost halfway there. I'm starting to get close.

OH NO! AHHH! THUD! OW.

I'm too lazy to walk that far.

Caelen Pittsley, Age 10

About the Author

I am turning 11 in about a month. I was born and spent the first 8 years of my life in central and northern California. I like writing and illustrating comic books.

P.S. I am not actually lazy.

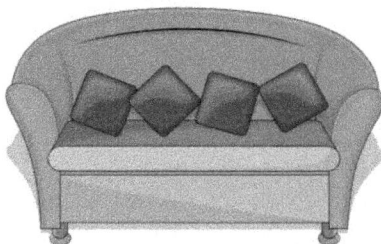

A Journey

Jungle
Outside
Us together on a trip
Roaming
Never say no to a journey
Expedition
Your journey

Alexis Torrey, Age 10

About the Author

Hello, my name is Alexis Torrey. I am in fifth grade, and I'm 10 years old. I was born in Everett, Washington; then I moved to Superior, Montana. I lived with my brother, grandma, grandpa, and pets. I have dogs, cats, and horses. I love Superior. I hope you enjoy reading my poem.

Hunting Wolves

Wolves

Three wolves on the hunt

Waiting, watching for their prey

Attack, they are off.

Oscar J. Wolff, Age 11

About the Author

My name is Oscar. I live in Superior, MT. I am 11 years old. I have three brothers and three sisters. My favorite subject is math, and my favorite summer activity is swimming.

Everlasting Adventure

Jumping far
Outdoor Experience
Up and away
Rising up
Never ends
Everlasting adventure
Youth learning
Simply the best

Heather Haskins, Age 10

About the Author

Hello, my name is Heather Haskins. I'm in fifth grade and I am the age of ten. I was born in Missoula but live in Torkio and go to school in Superior, MT. I live on a ranch with a bunch of horses, which are my favorite animals. I like writing things and poems are one of my favorite. When I write poems my hands go free and write what they want with some help from my head.

Journey Home

Dino running through the leaves.
I like the crunching sound.
Now we must go faster!
Ohhh we can't make it!
So we jump the river and catch a fish.
About time we get home.
Used to the crunching leaves I can no longer hear.
Roar!!!

Ani Hopwood, Age 10

About the Author

Hi. I'm Ani (On-nee) and I'm in 5th grade and almost 11. And I was born in Missoula. But my house is in Superior, and I've never moved. Thanks for taking time to read my poem. Thank you.

Sights and Feelings of a Journey

Journey
Obstacles
Universe
Rivers
Nervous
Exciting
Yonder

Abigail Wheeler, Age 10

About the Author

Hi, I'm Abigail Violet Wheeler. I'm 10 years old and go to Superior Elementary. I am in 5th grade. I love to write, read, and draw. Also, I'm really glad I entered the poem contest!

Journeys

Joyful
Outrageous
Useful in many ways
Rainy
Necessary
Excellent
Yearly

Memphis Vulles, Age 11

About the Author

Hi! My name is Memphis. I'm in 5th grade and I'm 11 years old. I'm from Superior, MT. I love graffiti, and I have brown-blonde hair and hazel eyes. Thank you for taking the time to read my poem!

Wolves

Wandering
Over
Logs
Victory
Eating
Snow shoe rabbit

Jackie Maxvill, Age 11

About the Author

Hi. My name is Jackie. I am 11 years old. I'm in 5th grade. I like it so far. I am from Superior, Montana, and I love animals but my favorite is a dog. My favorite subject in school is reading.

Diving

Diving

Endless water

Finding sharks everywhere

Taking all of my oxygen

Journeys

Joseph M. Wood, Age 10

About the Author

My name is Joseph. I was born in Waxahutchee, Texas and moved to Superior, Montana. I am in 5th grade. My favorite subject is math. I hope my poems get in the book so the other kids and adults can read them. Thank you.

Worms

Wondering where to go
On the move
Running on the sidewalk
Moving like crazy
Slithering

Addison Martin, Age 10

About the Author

Hello, my name is Addi. I'm in fifth grade. I'm originally from North Ogden, Utah. I really enjoy holding snakes and my snake. Also, I like reptiles and all animals. I love my farm also.

Journey Cinquain

Journey
Scary, Lonely
Jumping, Sprinting, Ducking
Only a little happiness
Travel

Abigail Wheeler, Age 10

Hi, I'm Abigail Violet Wheeler. I'm 10 years old and go to Superior Elementary. I am in 5th grade. I love to write, read, and draw. Also, I'm really glad I entered the poem contest!

DIFFERENT Journeys

Journeys
Outstanding journeys
Unique journeys to go on
Reptile journeys
Neighborhood journeys
Earthworm journeys
Yesterday's journeys
Ship journeys

Trina Azure, Age 11

About the Author

My name is Trina Joe Azure. I'm in 5th grade and I am 11 years old. I was born in Missoula, and I live in Superior, MT. I love reading poems. I go to Superior Elementary School. I have 1 sister and no brother.

Bob's Journey

There once was a frog named Bob.

Bob was a lonely frog.

Bob hopped and jumped, but couldn't find a friend.

Another frog came and they became friends.

The other frog's name is Bill.

So they played leapfrog.

Gracie Nicholson, Age 11

About the Author

My name is Gracie Nicholson. I am in fifth grade. I am 11 years old. I am from originally from Sundance, Wyoming. I live with 8 other people. Their names are Jannell (Mom), Donna (Aunt), Aria (cousin), Kadin (cousin), Alex (Brother), Wyatt (brother), Margaret (Grandma), Donald (Grandpa), Gracie (me), Buster (dog.)

Publisher's Prerogative

Eighteen

The girl in me
Plays and pretends.
The woman in me
A willful dream tends.

The child I am
Wills to be free.
The woman I am
A wife longs to be.

Youth so alive!
Comfort with age?
In spirit I've yet
To come to this page.

Eager and quick,
Calm like a rose.
Failure and hardships—
Yet still the soul grows.

To be eighteen—
The time of choice.
I learn with my ears.
I teach with my voice.

S. E. Thomas
© July 23, 1992

About Our Contest

The poems in this book were collected through a state-wide poetry contest entitled, "Into the Beautiful Poetry Contest." This is an annual contest open to artists of all ages. It begins September 1st and runs through October 15th. It is FREE to enter—which makes it perfect for individuals and for use as a class project for students of any age. There are three judging categories for poetry: Adult, Teen, and Child. Entrants compete only against those in his/her same category. For each category, we award first, second, and third place through a blind review process. We also acknowledge certain poems with an honorable mention.

(Neither the editor, nor her family are eligible to enter or win the contests; however, she has reserved the "Publisher's Prerogative" section at the back of the book to publish one poem.)

If you are interested in entering this contest or sharing this information with a teacher, a friend, or a family member, please bookmark the following informational resources:

Website: www.TheDramaticPen.com

Facebook: www.facebook.com/TheDramaticPen

Twitter: @TDPPress

Please sign up for our free, monthly e-newsletter through the home page on our website. All upcoming contests, calls for writers, and new products are announced there, as well as tips for writers, a book of the month, a tried and true recipe, and more! We hate junk mail as much as you do, so we promise not to fill up your inbox, and you can unsubscribe at any time.

About the Editor

S. E. Thomas, M.A.

is a multi-published, award-winning author, editor, and publisher. A wife, mother, and avid story-teller, she lives and works in Lolo, Montana. She has her master's degree in philosophy and writes biblical historical fiction, inspirational fiction, YA dystopia, Christian drama, and Christian non-fiction. She works at the local Care Net Pregnancy Resource Center. Susan is married to Dr. Aaron Thomas, and they have three children: Yesenia, Dakota, and Novik.

Please follow her author's page on Amazon and connect with her via Facebook and Twitter at:

www.facebook.com/AuthorSEThomas

@susanethomas1

More From:

@TDPPress
www.thedramaticpen.com
facebook.com/thedramaticpen

Into the Beautiful
Poetry by Montana Artists Series

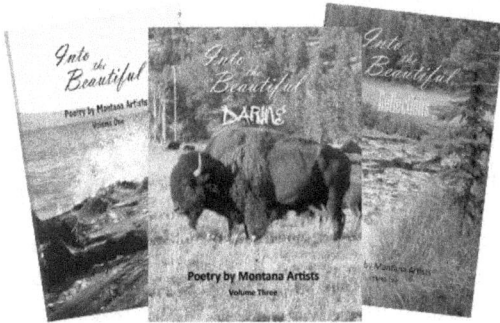

"Into the Beautiful: Poetry by Montana Artists" is a series of poetry books by Montana artists of all ages. These works of art and creativity were collected through annual contests run August through October 15th. To find out more about this contest, please visit our website at www.TheDramaticPen.com.

Longing for Rest
A Novella
S. E. Thomas

One heartbroken woman battles insomnia. Another cannot escape the coma trapping her between dreams and reality. Though they have never met, through a miraculous crossing of consciousness, they find themselves together on a grassy hill surrounded by a mysterious fog. In this dream world, Amy and Gracie form an unusual friendship. But will fear, pain, and betrayal follow them and spoil this haven? Will they finally be able to rest? Can a dream change your life? Available in paperback ($7.99) or eBook ($2.99 from Kindle or Nook.)

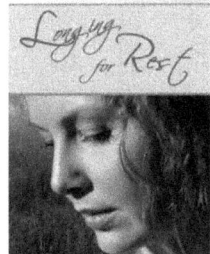

The Scrolls of the Nevi'im Series:

Book I: Habakkuk's Plea: A Prophet of Elohim
Book II: Habakkuk's Plea: Evil Persists
Book III: Habakkuk's Plea: Elohim Answers
S. E. Thomas

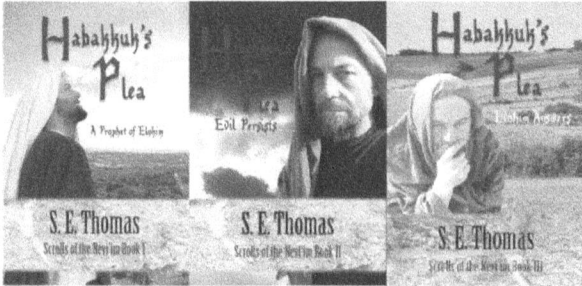

The Sixth Hour
Book I of the Holy Land Mysteries Series
S. E. Thomas

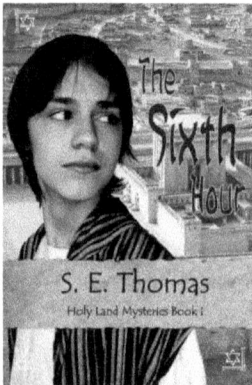

Can Darash, a Jewish teenager, track a killer, rescue his family from ruin, and discover the truth about Yeshua? The rebel, Yeshua, drove the merchants and moneychangers from the Temple with a whip. Hours later, one of them was murdered. Now fifteen-year-old Darash must find a way to protect his family from poverty even as he struggles with the grief of losing his father. When another murder is committed, Darash finds himself searching for a dangerous killer and relying on an old, blind basket-weaver for help. But will he be able to expose the killer before the killer finds him?

The Holy Land Mysteries Series
Darash's adventures continue with…

Book II: The Brazen Altar
Book III: The Mud Flower
And More!

Interactive Mystery Party Games
for Teens and Adults
S. E. Thomas

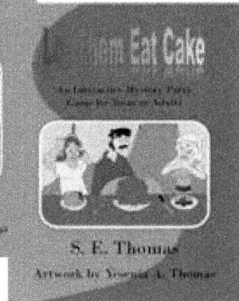

Who Invited the Stiff to Dinner?
Murder at Surly Gates
Accuracy
Let Them Eat Cake

A Reason To Celebrate
A Full-Length Christmas Production
S. E. Thomas

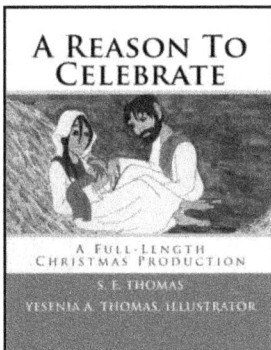

For most, Christmas is a time filled with joy. But for many, Christmas can be a difficult season. But let us consider a moment what Scripture tells us of the first Christmas. What really happened? For the first time, God Himself—the Creator of the Universe, the King of Kings, the Everlasting Father—stepped into our world! He stepped in— not to enjoy the wealth or the beauty or the joys—but to experience our suffering, our longings, and our sorrows. From the moment of His birth, He experienced far from ideal circumstances. Yet, we remember His words, "In this world you will have trouble. But take heart! I have overcome the world."

Acting Out Loud
Christian Skits for All Occasions
S. E. Thomas

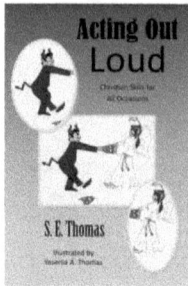

Whether you are a pastor looking for a skit to help drive home your message, a ministry leader desiring a dramatic reading to speak God's love at a retreat or conference, or a youth group leader hoping to spice up a youth meeting, we have the material you're looking for! Find over thirty skits, short plays, and dramatic readings that cover the following areas: Biblical Tales, Christian Living, Evangelism, Special Events, Holidays.

Lazy Dog
carol fields brown

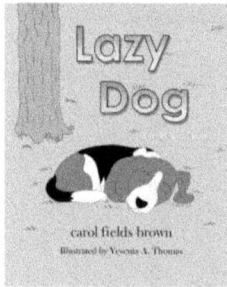

"The quick brown fox jumps over the lazy dog." This sentence is called a pangram. A pangram contains every letter of the English alphabet at least one time. This storybook starts with this famous pangram. The Lazy Dog and the Fox start us on an animal adventure. You can write the sentences and color the pictures. At the end of the book is a chart to help you make up your own sentences. At first you may need help, but soon you will be able to make your own. Every sentence can become a story. Do you know why the Fox jumped over the lazy dog? I wonder…. What do you think? This coloring book provides an opportunity for young learners to explore the intricacies of the English language, practice their handwriting, and explore a variety of animal behaviors in a fun and creative way. Full-color illustrations, matching coloring pages, and lines for handwriting practice are also included.

Sourdough Secrets… Revealed!
From Making the Starter to Sourdough Success!
Ray Templeton

Step-by-step instructions that will allow you to make your own starter, make your first loaf, and even learn to make sourdough bread in your bread machine.

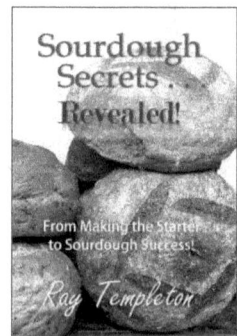

Is My Faith My Own?
A Resource for Christian Young People
Leaving Home for the First Time
S. E. Thomas

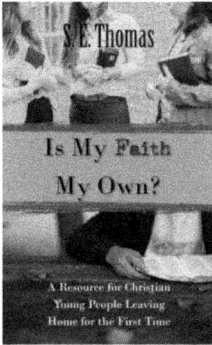

Everything was going along fine... then you got out on your own and realized it's your responsibility to get the rest of your life right. From here on out, if you're going to follow God, you're going to be doing it on your own. You can no longer coast by on your parents' faith, your pastor's understanding, or your youth leader's morals. Now it's up to you. And you have some questions: Is my faith real? Is it growing? Is it my own? (A *Finding Hope Resource Guide*.)

Complex Simplicity:
How Psychology Suggests Atheists are Wrong about Christianity
Dr. Lucian Gideon Conway III

In *Complex Simplicity*, prominent psychology researcher Dr. Lucian Gideon Conway III addresses the modern atheist attack on the psychological effectiveness of the Christian religion. As an expert in the science of cognitive complexity, Dr. Conway uses scientific research and personal narratives to argue that Christianity is an effective guide for reconciling the many complexities built into the human psyche. Directly contradicting what many modern atheists believe, he shows that, in approaching human psychology from a complex perspective, Christianity meets our complex needs with complex solutions. To Christian believers, he offers psychological reasons to believe their faith yields positive benefits. To skeptics, he offers a challenge to the growing cultural belief that Christianity is both simple-minded and ineffective. *Complex Simplicity* is important reading for anyone curious about the intersection of Christian teaching and human psychology.

www.ingramcontent.com/pod-product-compliance
Lightning Source LLC
Chambersburg PA
CBHW060039040426

42331CB00032B/1816